Youth Poetry Letters – Pe

Youth Poetry Letters

Dear Young Hearts,

You will one day work hard to fill oversized shoes, working to balance life. As you do, remember that the kindness flowing through your heart is immeasurable. It is filled with the sunshine of endless summers flourishing in dreams and possibilities. It shines brighter than the twinkling of the stars you wish upon at night, more profound than the ocean spread far before you, and more significant than the mountains you may one day want to climb.

Your viewpoints have not gone unnoticed, and we hope your heart grows larger and spreads. Your brand of magic is needed in this echo chamber called life, and we wish you all the stardust and wonder you can find in this world.

From a former kid, now a poet, disguised as a grown-up.

—Jacalyn Eyvonne

Youth Poetry Letters

Pencils and Dreams
Young Vallejo Poets Share Their World

Edited By
KATHLEEN HERRMANN AND JACALYN EYVONNE

Youth Poetry Letters, Pencils and Dreams, Young Vallejo Poets Share Their World.

Copyright 2024, Youth Poetry Letters. Jacalyn Eyvonne, Kathleen Herrmann. All Rights Reserved.
No part of this publication may be reproduced, distributed, or transmitted in any form or by any means, including photocopying, recording, electronic or mechanical methods, without prior written permission from the publisher, except in the case of brief quotations embodied in critical reviews, educational purposes, and specific other noncommercial uses permitted by copyright law.

Cover Design/Interior Artwork by
Jacalyn Eyvonne & Neuman Robinson, NeuImagery

For permission requests and information about bulk orders for schools, libraries contact us via
www.youthpoetryletters.com

ISBN 978-1-7354936-8-8 - Paperback
ISBN 978-1-7354936-9-5 - Hardcover

First Edition November 2024
Youth Poetry Letters, Vallejo, CA

Library of Congress Control Number: 2024921802

CONTENTS

Foreword	15
Natalie	17
Aranza	19
Delilah	20
Jonathan	22
Daniela	23
Sophia	24
AhiToki	26
Rico	27
Jayden	28
Alejandra	29
Marisol	30
Paul	31
CeCe	32
Nailea	33
Ryan	35
David	36
Joseph	37
Belle	38
Aaron	39
Brianna	40
Jared	41
Caridad	42
Timothy	44
Kayden	45
Sheila	46
Lailah	48

Alayna	49
Julieta	50
Quinton	51
Lionel	53
Emily	54
Eden	55
Mason	56
Aniyah	57
Isaiah	58
Ron	59
Jose	60
Catalina	62
Alma, *Time for Bed*	63
Jezebelle, *The Sunset*	64
Yarethzi, *Hop on Pop*	65
Jacob, *Family*	66
Sofia, *Family Time*	67
Flor, *Art*	68
Leslie, *My Dreams with Hello Kitty*	69
Isabella	71
David, *Talking Animals*	72
Alma, *Sick Day, Fruit, Fairy Tales*	73
Montisse, *Love*	76
Gia, *Fall*	78
Nicholas, *Summer*	80
Benji, *Monday Morning*	81
Tali, *A Boy and A Girl*	82

Ximena, *Halloween Is Here*	83
Sophia, *Halloween*	84
Aaron, *Christmas Feelings*	85
Orion	86
Hazel	87
Alma	89
Phoenix, *Strange Planet*	92
Kayden, *Dreams*	93
Jose, *The Haunted Tunnel*	94
Karla, *Describing Animals*	95
Kai, *Broccoli Donut Cloud Dream*	96
Alina, *A Tree*	97
Dane, *Space*	98
Paris, *My Rainbow*	100
Zakariya, *Basketball*	101
Sophia, *Leaves Falling*	102
Adrian, *My Imaginary Pet*	103
Eliana, *The Day Passes By*	104
Gage, *My First Things*	105
Vincent, *New York*	106
Kylie, *I See A Dog*	107
Soane, *I Love Fortnight*	108
Hazel, *Dream Life*	109
Cata, *Rain Rain, Go Away*	111
Kali, *A Dog Who Loves Rain*	112
Alma, *Rainstorm*	113
Dayana, *I See God*	114
Messiah, *Space*	115
Victoria, *Art Time!*	116
Leini, Fish, *Sky*	117
Alex, Soccer	118

Valeria, *Beach Sunset*	119
Samantha, *Me and My Dog*	120
Leslie, *Fall Fun*	121
Aileen, *Float*	122
Nathalia, *My Kitty*	124
Kenneth, Soccer	125
Jayla, *Birds and Butterflies*	126
David, *Little Brother*	127
Anita, *Me!*	128
Juan, *School Dreams*	129
Noah, *My Gaming Dream*	130
Julian, *The Pool*	131
Xavier	132
Biographies	133
Kathleen Herrmann	134
Jacalyn Eyvonne	136
Vallejo Teaching Artists (VTA)	138

**Let your words
be the source used
to paint the world
as you see it.**

FOREWORD

Between its covers, this book holds the words of children. You will hear their voices, playful spirits, deep thoughts, endless wonder, and things that bring them joy.

This anthology reflects the talent and potential of our Vallejo youth. It is my hope to give all young artists, writers, filmmakers, dancers, and musicians a space for their creativity to be shared and valued by the whole community. In that spirit, I know you will treasure this collection of poems for years to come.

Renay Conlin
Director, Vallejo Center for the Arts

This project is the product of a collaboration between Vallejo Teaching Artists and Co-Poets Laureate Jacalyn Eyvonne and Kathleen Herrmann.

Natalie
Grade 3, Age 8

When I go see the ocean, I feel excited.
I watch as the ocean laps loudly on the rocks.
When I grow up, I want to be a scuba diver
so I can see and find out the secrets
of the watery ocean below.

Sometimes, I see fish of different shapes, sizes,
and colors. It makes me calm and imaginative!
Sometimes, I pick up rainbow seashells.
It is so much fun to be out in the sun at the water.
Sometimes, I feel like the ocean is my home!
When I was little, I did not like the ocean.
But now I am fond of the ocean.
Blue! Blue is my favorite color.

I pick up plastic trash from beaches.
Trash can be bad for the environment,
especially the ocean.
It can affect fish and sea turtles.
They think plastic bags are jellyfish, so they eat it.
They can get sick, and yes, they can die.
That is why I take care of the ocean.
I love the ocean.

Aranza
Grade 3, Age 8

I love going to the beach.
It's fun to read.
Sometimes I bring my car.
I like going at the sunset.
The sunset is a little orange,
yellow, blue, and pink.
It's fun to play on the sand.
Sometimes I go to the beach
with my aunty. She is 16.
She can drive. I love her.
If the sea is clean,
sea animals are going to be safe.
Some animals eat jellyfish.
Plastic bags look like jellyfish
That is why I NEVER!! EVER!!
Throw trash at the sea.

Delilah
Grade 3, Age 8

I got a dog. I saw a cat break into my house.
My mom had a cat and a dog. Wow!
The dog used the floor as a toilet.
I clean up, but my cat keeps making a mess.
A man hit the poor kitty.
The dog ate all my treats.
The dog jumped on me, and 20 cats
attacked the man.
The cat chased me, and I found out
that the cat needed food, so I adopted him.
The dog attacked the cat.
The dog jumped in a hole.
Oh, no!
I can call the fireman to save the dog.
The cat pushed my dog into the hole.
Then I took a hammer to fix my bed,
but my dog jumped on me,
and the bed broke on me.
Ow!
I said, "bad dog!"
The dog learned his lesson
when I put him in the cage.

I call the builder,
and I pay 1,000 dollars,
and the builder said, "I'm rich!"

I said, "Get out!" "Come back, Emily!"
I said, "You're being bad. Get in the cage, now!"
Where is my dog? "Hey, put my dog down.
You're a thief!"
He said, "okay, fine."
"Now get out!" I said.
"Hi, Emily. Wanna play fetch?"
The dog shook her head.
"Let's go for a walk," I said.
I put the leash on, but the dog pulls hard.
"Ahhh!"
I fall on the ground.
"I'm going to play a prank on you.
Boo!"
The dog was scared.
Ha, ha!

Jonathan
Grade 3, Age 8

**I went to my mom's room,
and I got into my mom's bed.
I saw a black cat.
I was nervous
it would attack my dog.**

Daniela
Grade 3, age 8

I have a fake sister.
I feel a lot of feelings.
One is happy because
I do nothing with her.
She lives far away.

Sophia
Grade 3, Age 8

There's a couple in Paris
who want to take a love picture.
Their names are Mia and Max.
They say, "Let's take a picture
to remember this perfect day,"
so they try the beautiful Eiffel Tower,
but it was too crowded, so they say, "No!"
Then they try a waterfall.
It was too noisy. They say, "No! No!"
Finally, they find the perfect place.
An artist paints their picture.
They say, "This is the perfect picture."

AhiToki
Grade 3, Age 8

I was watching TV, and my dad gave a cute baby cat to me and my sibling. The cat was so hungry. I fed the cat so the cat wouldn't starve. The next day, I showed my cousin JJ the cat. The cat loved my cousin and ran off until he came back with his dog. The cat did not like the dog at all! It scratched the dog. After I grabbed the cat away from the dog, the cat had sharp nails. The cat started scratching me. It didn't hurt at all. The next day, my grandma said she saw the cat running all over the living room. I went to the backyard to play. My cousin came, and the cat ran away hiding. We had an idea. We got cat food. It took a while, but it was worth it because the cat came back. Then it hid under my dad's tools. It took so long to get her.

Rico
Grade 3, Age 8

My dog is fast.
She keeps up with my fast,
flying toy.
It goes five miles per hour.
She has a five-inch tail.
She likes to wag it.
She's eight years old.
She is really tall.
I love her.
She is cute.
I'll do anything for her.
I'll make sure she never gets hurt.

Jayden
Grade 3, Age 8

I went to China.
I met this boy.
He asked me if he could have some chow.
Then I ask him if he's hungry.
He says yes.
Then we eat some dumplings and noodles.
I go to his house and play checkers.
I go back to America and got to sleep.
I remember how I was nervous
when I saw the boy,
happy when I had chow,
joyful when he offered me dumplings
and noodles with the chow.

Alejandra
Grade 3, Age 8

Peaceful Place
Flower
Green, brown, red, pink—rose tree
Wind blowing

Dog
Black, cute, playful, fluffy
Run, run

Nature
Bush to bush, green and beautiful

Family
Mom, dad, joy, smile
That's my mom

Grandma, grandpa
Nice, loving, safe, sweet

Tree
Rest in peace
Swing, swing, happy in fall leaves

Marisol
Grade 3, Age 8

Unicorn Dreams
I see unicorns in picture books and sometimes in chapter books.
I feel joy reading.
I dream of having a unicorn and that makes me happy.
I want to be friends with a unicorn.
We can have ice cream and hot chocolate.
I'm too excited to wait.
I want to sleep with a unicorn.
We can share a room and that brings me joy.
I want to ride a unicorn to school and to the park.
I feel so happy when I read books on unicorns.

Paul
Grade 3, Age 8

I drive to the place, get dressed in the bathroom,
and jump into the cold water. I eat food.
The last thing I do is jump into the pool again.
Then I swim back to my house.
My mom got me a black towel
because the sun didn't dry me.
I went to my bed.

Cece
Grade 3, Age 8

I'm going to tell you about me and my sissy.
She is funny. I am funny, too.
We love to watch TV, and we are happy.
We are the best sisters ever.
I love her; she is cool.
I see her every day.
She likes Crayola pink.
I like Crayola blue.
We like to go to the park
and she says, "My name is Cece!"

Nailea
Grade 3, Age 8

I am proud to be in Girl Scouts.
The name is gsnorcal.org.
When we go inside, we stand up
and say something to help the world.
My leader says, "We are having a good day today."
We are going to sell Girl Scout Cookies this
summer. We are going camping this summer, too.
We got a songbook. We have been practicing the
songs, and they are really funny.
We are going to make cookies.
I'm going to make mint.
Sometimes, we eat snacks like goldfish
and talk about feelings.
We do talents, so I did dancing.
I love to listen to Taylor Swift.
Last Tuesday, we said happy birthday
because it was Girl Scouts 112th birthday.
Back then, it was just Boy Scouts,
and the women wanted Girl Scouts.
Then the woman who made the Girl Scouts died, so
we wrote, "Happy birthday to Girl Scouts,
you made this place better."

Ryan
Grade 3, Age 8

So, I was at my auntie Jasmine's house, and a crack was underneath it. Lizards would think that's their home, so my cousin likes to catch them. So, one day, I gave him an idea. I said, "Let's catch one and make it our pet." So, he caught it, and we trapped it in a plastic cup.

David
Grade 3, Age 8

My cousin tells me there is a lizard.
I start to walk over. Then it runs.
It looks at me for a couple of seconds.
I was thinking, why was it there?
I think it wondered what I was.
It jumped in the water.

Joseph
Grade 3, Age 8

I wake up.
Then I go into the living room.
Next, my dog does a dance for me!
Then I feed him dog food and water.
Next, I get ready for school.
I say goodbye to my dog.
It makes me super happy.
I feel like he has a love for me
that can never end.
It's sad to leave him because
we love each other.
He is so cute when he does his dance.
I love my dog so much.
I walk to the car, get in,
and my dad drives me to school.

Belle
Grade 3, Age 8

I have a favorite superhero.
I like to call her mom.
I love her so much.
She is always there.
She always cares.
And I'm always going to care about her.

She always makes me feel
loved, happy, and calm.
Sometimes, my mom
can make me a little mad.
I repeat SOMETIMES.
My mom never gives up.
When she gives up, I give up.

She always tries her best,
and that makes me try my best.
I am so grateful for my mom.
What I want to say straight to her face is
I love you so much.
I will ALWAYS love you the way I do now.
I want to be like you!

Aaron
Grade 3, Age 8

I go to the sandy beach.
Then I saw the huge
blue and white ocean.
I hear a beautiful sound
in the distance.
I feel shocked.
Then, when I walk closer,
the sound turns louder and louder.
I hear swish, swish, swish
along the ocean breeze.
After that, I hear
splash, splash, splash.
The waves are crashing
into each other loudly.
I feel happy
when the cold breeze
crashes into me.
It feels cold.

Brianna
Grade 3, Age 8

My best friend's name is Antonella Hembra Sapiens. Her favorite colors are pink, blue, and purple. Antonella was born here, but she speaks Spanish. Antonella has two dogs. One is a French bulldog named Chicken, but in Spanish, it's Pollo. The other is a chihuahua. Her dogs are joyful. She will always be my bestie.

I have nicknames for her, Angel and Bestie. She calls me Stitch, Bestie, Bri, and Bri-Bri. We like to get ice cream together. I like strawberry, chocolate, vanilla, and bubble gum. She likes the same ice cream that I like! Me and her almost like the same things. She likes it when I go to her house. Antonella makes me feel loved, special, and happy. I love the fact she's very funny. Also, I love how she's caring. When I fall, she doesn't laugh. She helps me up.

But I don't like it when she copies me. Also, I don't like it when she rolls her eyes at me and yells at me. When she yells at me, it hurts my feelings. Also, sometimes we fight and yell. After 1 minute, we're friends again.

Jared
Grade 3, Age 8

My two dogs have two beds.
The boy is age 2.
The girl is age 1.
We live in an apartment.
My two dogs have two toys.
My dogs always come to my room,
take my toys, hide my toys.
It makes me happy.

Caridad
Grade 3, Age 8

A little black spider.
It wouldn't stop following me.
It was creepy.
I was confused and nervous.
I was finishing my missing work,
and I forgot my pencil.
No matter what I did,
it wouldn't stop following me.
Then I walked over a crack.
The spider could not get over the crack.

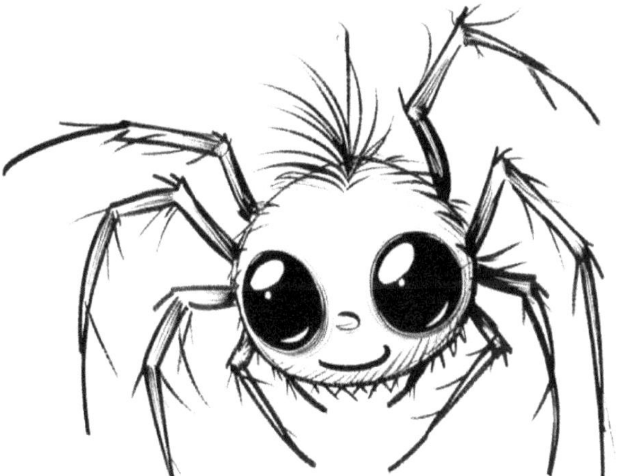

Timothy
Grade 3, Age 8

I go to the playground.
I play on the rainbow thing on the slide
and I run with my friends.
Going on the slide and running
are my favorite things to do.
Run, run, run, slide, slide, slide.
When I go on the slide,
it feels like I am flying like a bird.
It feels like a dream.
The wind blows on my face.
I love recess.

Kayden
Grade 3, Age 8

I ride my roller skates in the park.
I eat a snack on the bench.
Then I play on the playground.
I finish riding my roller skates in the park.
My roller skates feel soft.
When I ran in my roller skates,
I say, "Chockobro dude!"
I feel strong in my heart.

Sheila
Grade 3, Age 8

I like sorbet and relaxing and sleeping.
I like to be with my family, to do homework,
and be with my friends. I also like pizza,
the pool, being with my dog.
I like to write a lot, and I also like school.
I like to play with my sister and call my friends.
I like to travel to El Salvador,
and I'm going to live in Merilan.
I like the beach in the summer.
I like all the fruits, coloring, and drawing,
and going out a lot.
I would like to be with my dad, who died.
I like Stitch and Angel and the toys,
and the black table.
I like to take care of my sister and read the books
that are called <u>Dog Man and the Babysitters</u>.
I already read part one,
and I am in part two of <u>Dog Man</u>.
I like my family.

Me gusta el sorbete y relajante es dormir. Me gusta estar con mi familia y hacer tarea, y estar con mis amigas. Me gusta la pizza y la piscina y estar con mi perrito y llamarles a mis amigas. Me gusta escribir mucho y también me gusta la escuela. Me gusta jugar con mi hermana y llamarles a mis amigas. Me gusta viajar à El Salvador y yo me voy a ir a vivir à Merilan. Me gusta la playa el verano. Me gusta todas las frutas y colorear y dibujar mucho y también salir mucho. Me viera gustado estar con mi papa que se murió. Me gusta Stitch y Angel y los juguetes y me gusta la mesa con nielo y me gusta cuidar à mi hermana y leer los libros que se llaman <u>Hombre Perro Y Las Niñas De La </u>Niñera. Yo leí la parte uno estoy en la parte dos del <u>Hombre Perro</u>. Me gusta mi familia.

Lailah
Grade 3, Age 8

One day, I walked in the woods.
I looked at the flowers.
I sat in the field.
I looked out at the trees,
and I felt a breeze,
"Swoosh! Swoosh!"
It sounds quiet.
I looked back at the trees,
and I looked at the leaves.
The leaves look cool,
the field feels soft,
the trees sound calm,
the woods feel safe.
When I look at Nature,
I feel calm and peaceful.
It feels like home.

My dad and my grandma make me feel safe because they let me play and swim in Nature. They make me s'mores. I feel safe with them because they watch out for me in case I get hurt. I feel beauty in Nature.

Alayna
Grade 3, Age 8

My Grandma lives in Mexico. I love her so much. My Grandma's pet birds are named Rosa and Livi. They are love birds. My Grandma's dogs are cute. She has five. My Grandma and I are so happy to see each other. We love making tamales, going to the ice cream store, and eating ice cream. She watches me when I ride her horse. I feel cool and happy. I love going to Mexico to see my Grandma. It's a special moment because she lives in Mexico. It's rare to see her.

Julieta
Grade 3, Age 8

The phone starts to ring.
Ring, ring!
I get up from doing my homework,
pick up the phone.
My mom tells me that my grandmother
passed away. I drop the phone.
I am shocked. I start to cry.
My brother asked me what had happened.
I tell him that Grandmother passed away.
He starts to tap my back. I am crying.
He asks me if I am hungry. I say yes.
He starts to make the food.
I finish my homework and my food.
I give him a hug and say thank you.
We hug each other.

Quinton
Grade 3, Age 8

**I have a cat in Hawaii.
I eat ice cream in Hawaii.
And Timothy is there.
But I want to go to space.
I will fly to Pluto.**

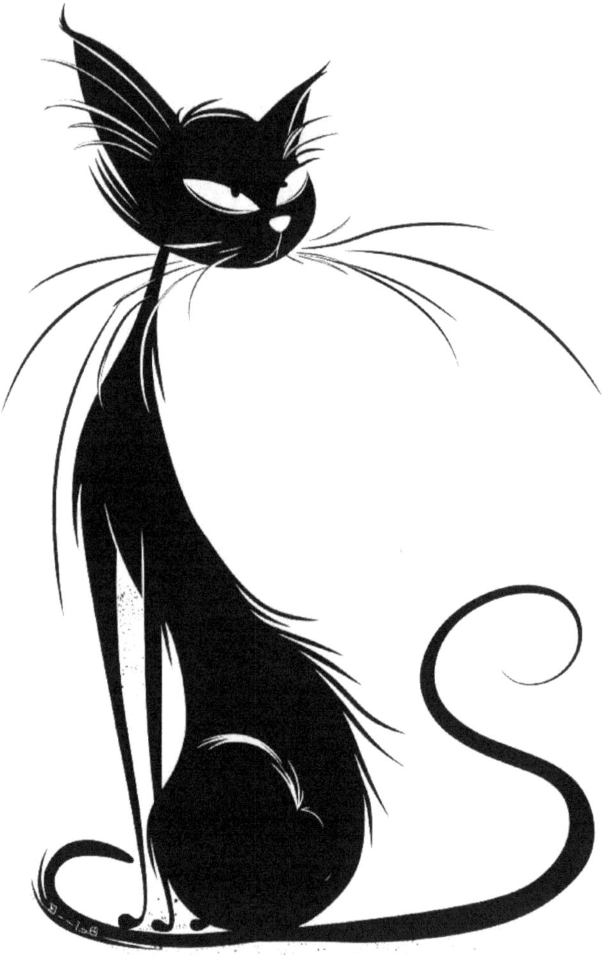

Lionel
Grade 3, Age 8

I rode my bike. Then I saw a cat.
I popped a wheelie. I was drifting.
I was scared because I almost hit the cat.
I pushed my brake down, and my bike stopped.
The cat ran away.
I was scared I was going to hit the cat
because I was going so fast.
Yes, I did feel relieved. I didn't hit the cat.

Emily
Grade 3, Age 8

I have a cousin. Her name is Alexis.
I've known her for six years.
She is two years older than me, so she is 11.
She is funny. I go to her house on Sundays,
but not every Sunday. She's nice to me.

Sometimes she is mean, which I don't like.
She kind of ignores me for some reason,
but overall, she is a really nice, kind cousin.
She says nice stuff and spends
a lot of time with me, and makes sure I'm happy
most of the time. We have the same opinions on
things. She is my favorite cousin.

Eden
Grade 3, Age 8

A new kid comes to school. He was nine years old.
I was nervous to ask him to be my friend.
My heart was pounding, boom, boom, boom.
I asked him. He said yes! I am so excited.
The next day, we played tetherball together.
In August, he invited me to his party.
When I got to his house, Emiliano came to the
party, too. Genaro said it was his brother's party.
I was curious how old his brother was turning.
Genaro said, "one year old." My mind was blown.
Boom, boom! I said, "My sister is three years old."
I got lots of candy. His brother opened my present.
He loved the Legos I gave him. I was happy he
liked it. Then, when I was going to leave, Genaro
said, "Thanks for coming." I was sad to leave,
but I had fun with my new friend.

Mason
Grade 3, Age 8

I used to be afraid of this dog until I fed it.
We became friends. It made me feel happy.
It was the best thing that happened in my life.
Every time I see the dog, it runs to me,
excited to see me. Even when I am sitting down,
it runs to me because it always wants to play.
It loves bacon treats, but it will eat human food,
lettuce, fries, even pasta with a secret ingredient.
I know the dog loves me because it always runs to
me with excitement. It's the best dog in the world.

Aniyah
Grade 3, Age 8

One day, I went to the park. The sky was so beautiful. I was playing on the slide and swings. "It's so fun," I said. I even made new friends. It was so exciting! I even had a BBQ and ate BBQ chicken because it was my sister's birthday. I had so so so much fun. We went home, opened the presents, and ate cake. I had the best day ever. When it started to turn night, we watched a movie, a scary movie, and made popcorn.
It was the best time of my life.

Isaiah
Grade 3, Age 8

One day,
I wanted to try a new game
called Fall Guys.
I think about what the game is like:
click, click, click.
I'm in my first game.
I'm racing to the finish line, and
there is one more spot open.
I cross it just in time.
I'm in the last round.
Two people left "bonk!"
One more person!
We're both tired.
Oops! I fell off, and I lost.
I'm really mad, but I can try again.

Ron
Grade 3, Age 8

I hesitate if I should go out there to Samoa.
I am going to be scared, but I am so curious.
My dad says the spiders are bigger than his hand.
You can see the bottom of the water. I am grateful
my cousin lives there. Samoa is very small.
I want to meet my Grandpa's twin. My sister says
he is very nice. My Dad says he was a teacher,
so he probably knows a lot and will ask me
questions. My Grampy can also show me around
the place. I will sleep, but not in a place with a lot
of bugs. I will catch a lizard or gecko. Well, I will
try! If I scream, I will shock them because they will
move.
We will have our reunion in Samoa. I am so excited
to go there. I will miss it when I go back to my
house because I will miss my Grandpa's twin and
my cousin.

Jose
Grade 3, Age 8

Me and sister went to the park.
We slide, "Weeee!"
We saw a duck.

She had babies.
She was looking for food for them.
Their species eat spiders, ants, and worms.
I found worms. I gave them to the duck.

Mom says, "Time to go home."
On Friday, I'll come back and help the duck.

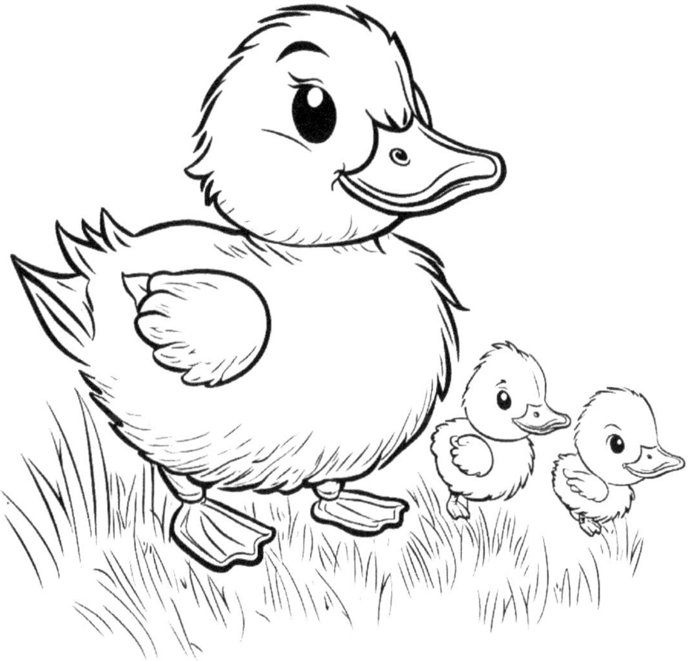

Catalina
Grade 3, Age 8

It all started with my twin cousin.
I was so excited to go to Alaska with her.
The only reason why I went to Alaska
is because of our birthdays.
We went to dinner, ice skating, and shopping.
My twin cousin is nice, beautiful, and joyful.
I feel good to have a twin cousin.
It makes me so happy.
My birthday is next month on May 30.
I wonder if we can go to the mall together.

Alma
Age 8

Time For Bed
Glittery paint in my room
The sound of raindrops outside
My mom's footsteps on the stairs
Goodnight kisses
Time for bed

Jezebelle
Grade 3, Age 8

The Sunset
I see sunset,
Pretty red, orange, yellow.
All the animals come to see
the pretty sunset in the sky.
I was so happy.
I love that the animals
come to see it.
They sleep on my lap.
When I see the moon,
it is time to sleep.
Then I sleep with them.

Yarethzi
Grade 3, Age 8

Hop On Pop
Hop on Pop
I like to hop on pop
Come on everyone, let's hop on pop
It is going to be really fun
Ms. Pink and Mr. Blue, would you like to jump on pop?
Sure!
"That is so fun!" Ms. Pink and Mr. Blue said.
Pop woke up and said, "get off me!"

Jacob
Grade 3, Age 8

Family
My grandma
is the best grandma in the world.
I want to hug her when she comes.
I miss her.
She's important to me.
If she dies,
I will start crying.
I wish I can see her again.
She's coming on her birthday
to visit me.
I am happy.
My wish is coming true.
What to do about family around the world?

Sofia
Grade 3, Age 8

Family Time
My big sister is so kind
Instead of saying hi to her friends first,
　she says hi to me
I always say hi to my little sis because
I love her, and I hope she is safe with
　me
My brother is tall, kind, and funny
He cares about me and hugs me
My parents are so important to me
Me and all my family watch movies
I love family time

Flor
Grade 3, Age 8

Art
I love art
When I do a drawing, it's cute
Art is for all kids to do
Art is something I can do my best
Sometimes I do not do good things on my art
When I am done, I show my pictures
to the people in my house
They ask, how many hours did it take?
I say, sometimes five thousand!
They say, everything you do
with your hands is special to us
I love my art

Leslie
Grade 3, Age 8

My Dreams with Hello Kitty!
Meet Hello Kitty.
She's cute, pink and white,
and looks like a princess!
I dream of going to the Hello Kitty
cafeteria with my cousins.
We would also go to the beach
with Hello Kitty.
We went to the party with her friends.
I dress like Hello Kitty.
We will be twins.
That's me saying bye.
My eyes teared up.
I didn't want to leave.
It is so fun to spend the day
with Hello Kitty.

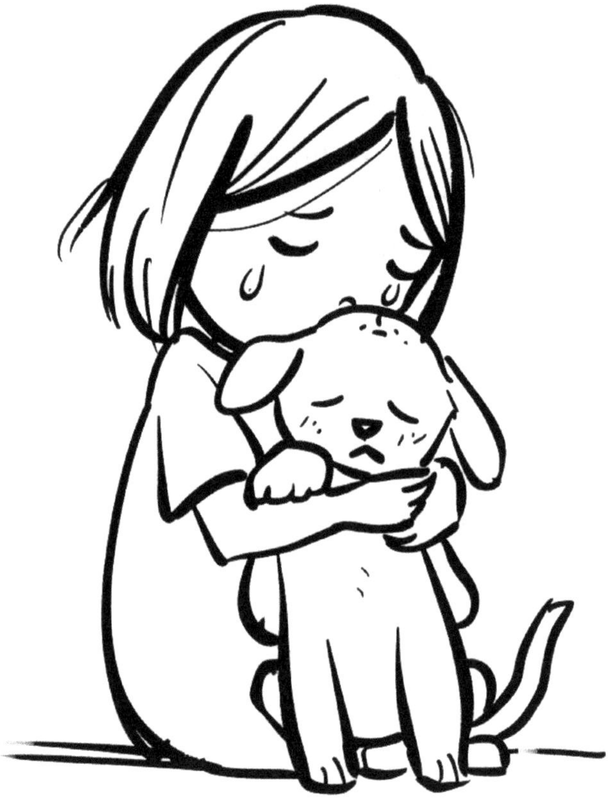

Isabella
Grade 3, Age 8

My dog was sick. I was so scared.
My dog made me happy.
We put honey in her water.
I let her sleep.
She laid down for a long time.
I was sad. Her sister was sad
because she had never been alone.
She was the love of her sister.
The next day she stopped breathing.
We took her to get buried.
We miss her, how crazy and funny she was.
If you want to know her name, you can ask me.
I still love her so much.

David
Grade 3, Age 8

Talking Animals
I hear animals talking
I talk to a tiger named Tile.
Me and Tile go to Tile's home
The jungle
I met Tile's family
It was very fun
Bye Tile
I will see you again in my imagination

Alma
Age 8, YPL Workshop Student

Sick Day
Sound of your mom coming up the stairs
You tell her you feel sick,
and she lets you stay home
Sound of your stomach rumbling
You take a nap

Alma
Age 8, YPL Workshop Student

Fruit

Fruit is juicy,
fruit is yummy
Fruit is soft and hard,
ripe and not
I will always love fruit

Alma
8th Grade, YPL Workshop Student

Fairy Tales
Mermaids, dragons
and mythical creatures
are what people call myths
But anything can be real

All those creatures could exist.

Montisse
8th Grade, YPL Workshop Student

LOVE
Love.
Love is happiness.
Love is like a field of dandelions.
Love is feeling at peace.
Love is like the feeling you get when you
take that first bite of your favorite food.
Love is happiness.

But love can also be sadness.
It'll have its ups and downs because
nothing, and nobody's perfect.
So, it's up to you to decide whether or not
you wanna fix the problem or give up.
With that being said, whatever you do,
just know that love never fails.
If it fails, it was never love.

I would always try to love other people
or be loved by them,
But I always ended up disappointed.
Then I'd wonder why.
Why can't I be loved?
Why can't I love?
Then I finally realized what was missing.

And that was self-love.
Because how do you expect to love or be loved if you don't even love yourself?

Gia
Grade 8, Age 13

Fall
Fall is soon
Feel the breeze
Leaves turn orange
Nights get longer
Things to look forward to
I love the fall

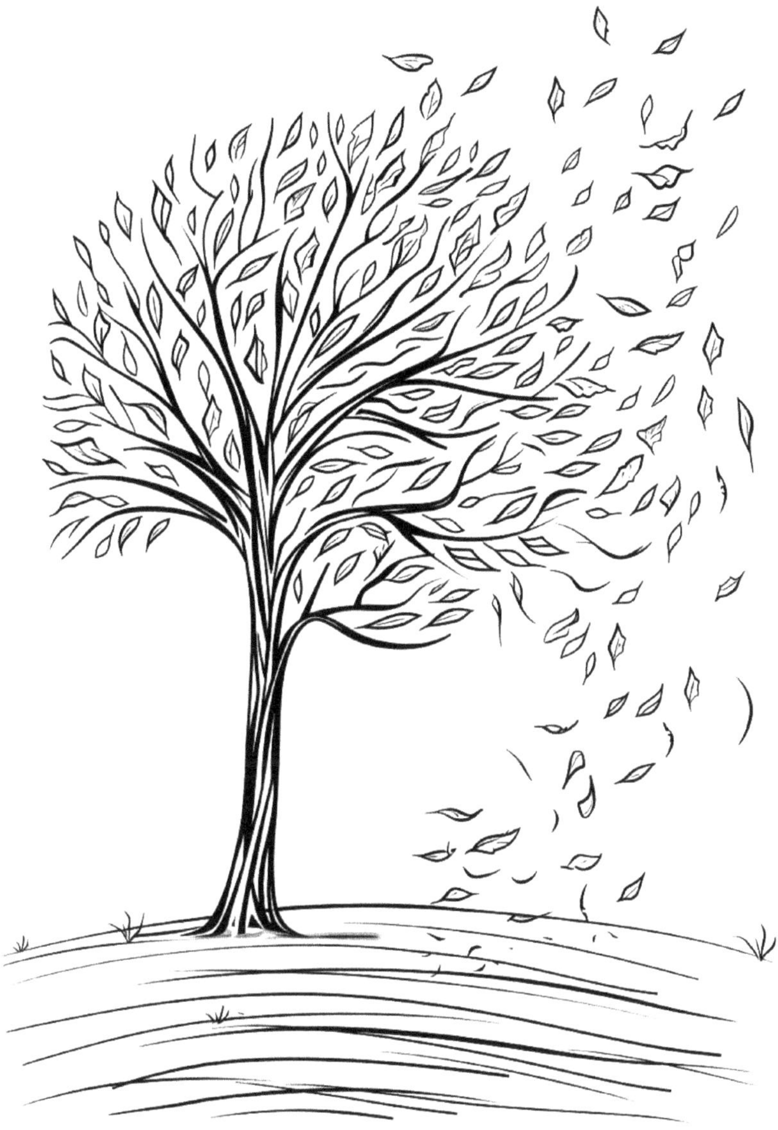

Nicholas
Grade 8, Age 13

Summer
Summer is the feeling of you in the pool swimming
while other people are sweating at their job
When you eat carne asada at the beach
Sometimes sand gets in your mouth
Sleeping in the air is refreshing,
just like the smell of the ocean
Eating cold food cool
Bees flying around being bees, pollinating
Airport being full
and every ticket to Hawaii is booked
Feeling breeze on a summer day is like
finding a needle in a haystack
I see people swimming
and I imagine myself in the water
I hear all different kinds of music,
enjoying the moment
The water is cold at the beginning
Just like winter, you get used to the cold
and have fun in the water
In summer, everyone is living in the moment.

Benji
Grade 8, Age 13

Monday Morning
I wake up
I go to school
I go to sleep
I'm in a loop and waiting change
Until today
Something changed

Tali
Grade 8, Age 13

A Boy and A Girl
A boy and a girl meet
They start hanging out
Scott is in a band and he plays the bass
Scott loves Ramona but she has
something to tell him
Scott has to fight her evil exes
Scott struggles but soon defends himself
from all of them
Scott and Ramona live happily ever after

Ximena
Grade 8, Age 13

Halloween Is Here
I wake up one chilly day
My costume comes in handy
I grab my basket
I see people come out of a casket
I go home and see a gnome
I lay it on my bed
And say "Goodnight Halloween!"
And then I hear a loud scream

Sophia
Grade 8, Age 13

Halloween
Halloween is my favorite holiday
The night of October 31st
Kids go door to door in different costumes
Saying "Trick or Treat!"
The smell of candy through the air
My candy basket swinging
I collect full-size candy bars

Aaron
Grade 8, Age 13

Christmas Feelings
Christmas looks like stockings by the chimney,
Christmas trees, beautiful moments
Christmas sounds like movies and giggling
I taste the tamales my mom makes for parties
I feel the warm, soft blankets in my bed
I smell the cold, fresh winter air
I feel cozy because I stay home and watch movies
Christmas makes me feel the most comfortable of any time in the whole year

Orion
Age 7, YPL Workshop Students – Vallejo

Cats do not eat bees
Yes, dogs eat bees
Cats are more cautious than dogs
It makes no sense
Cats have smaller brains than dogs
I'm confused

Hazel
Age 9, YPL Workshop Student

**Life is hard
Life can be sadder than death
Happiness is love**

Hazel
Age 9, YPL Workshop Student

Waterfalls are beautiful
They hold power, and they are strong
But they can also be stopped if you find the river or stream
It's coming
You can stop it by putting rocks
But you shouldn't stop waterfalls
You could get hurt or mess up the way the river flows

Alma
Age 9, YPL Workshop Student

I remember when my mom forgot me
at the sushi restaurant
I was so sad
I was surprised she didn't see
when I didn't come in the car
Next time, I would go straight to the car
I don't want to be left behind
I won't have any water or food
and I'll be very scared

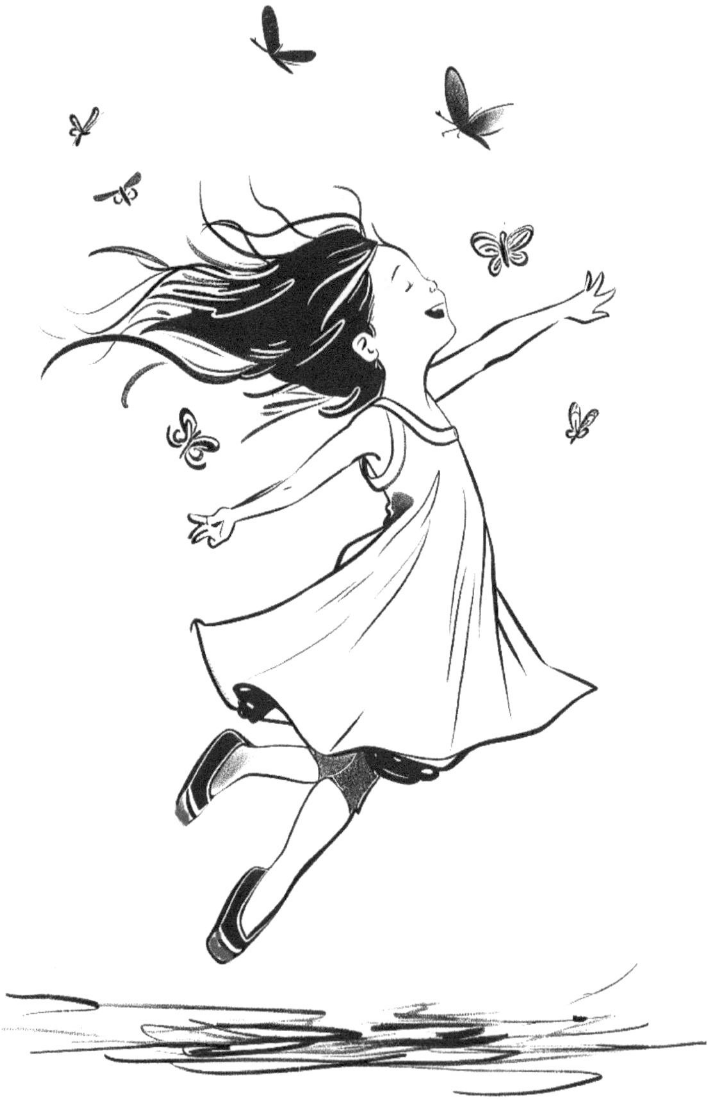

Alma
Age 9, YPL Workshop

Butterflies have very fragile wings
Butterflies are very beautiful
Butterflies need a humid habitat to live
Butterflies are amazing creatures
They can fly so high in the air
I feel like I've seen something special

Phoenix
Grade 3, Age 8

Strange Planet
I landed on this strange planet.
I'm excited to explore.
The leaves are purple,
the roses are blue,
the grass is red,
and the sky is green.
It has aliens and an animal
who looks like a cat's head
mixed with a dog's head.
The city looks futuristic.
The cars fly, and the planes drive.
It is time to go home. I liked that planet.
I hope I can go there again.

Kayden
Grade 3, Age 8

Dreams
I dream about being so rich
And flying in a private jet
through white puffs and blue sky
Reno is one minute from home
Do you want to travel to New York, N.J.?
I hope he says yes
It will be exciting!

Jose
Grade 3, Age 8

The Haunted Tunnel
When I come in, I see a big,
furry black widow spider on a wall
I hear someone screaming
A ghost touches my hand
I feel scared
I have to eat
So, I lick some hot Cheetos.

Karla
Grade 3, Age 8

Describing Animals
I see animals everywhere I go
I see some that are small
and some that are big
like in school. I see cats in the park
Some eat leaves like a giraffe,
some eat trash like a racoon,
some even eat beef like a wolf
or a raccoon or a giraffe
You could eat some, like a pig, but not all
Some are fluffy, some are spiky
Some are mammals, but some are reptiles
like a turtle
Some are birds like a peacock,
oh-uh-oh-uh-oh
Some are one color;
some are multiple colors
like a hummingbird, but not a lion
Some birth underwater and out of it too,
like a crocodile
Last are my feelings
I feel thankful to animals like bees.

Kai
Grade 3, Age 8

Broccoli Donut Cloud Dream
I see me and my mom below the clouds
I dream that me and my brother are
 on top of the clouds with donuts and broccoli
We eat them
They taste yummy and delicious
We fly over the cloud on a plane, joyful, so joyful
We land, leave the plane
That was fun
I'm feeling so excited for my next journey

Alina
Grade 3, Age 8

A Tree
I see a tree
I wish I am in a tree
I see a cat in a tree
I see a home
I see the sky
She was dreaming of a tree

Dane
Grade 3, Age 8

Space
I see space up in the sky
I dream that I touch the moon and touch Uranus
I see the moon and stars up in the sky
In the spaceship, I see all the planets
On the moon, I see the Earth, a big blue ball
I feel so excited

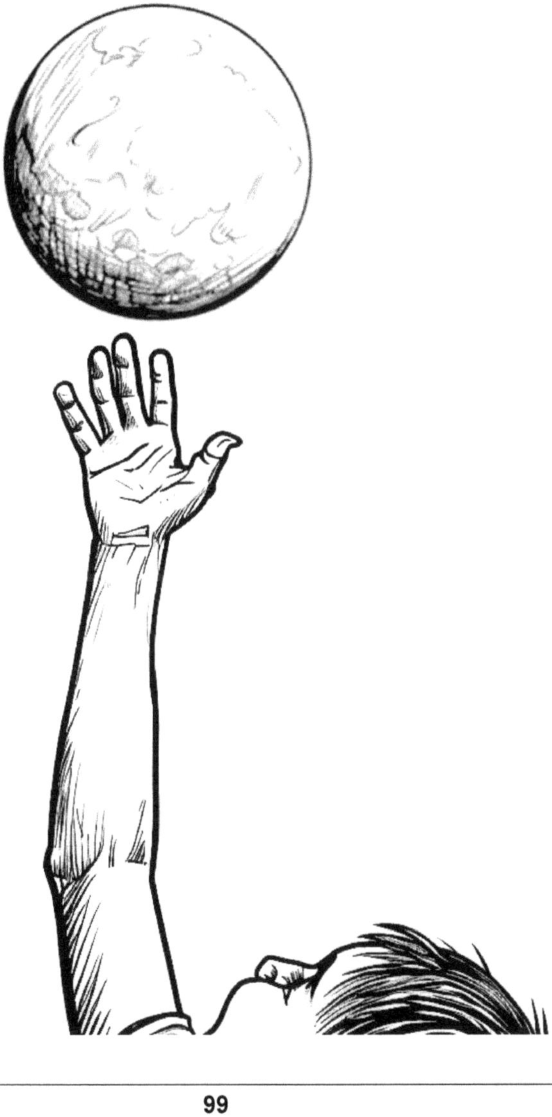

Paris
Grade 3, Age 8

My Rainbow
When I look up,
I see a rainbow
I see colors
I hear the birds humming
I taste the rainbow
I touch clouds
I look up at my world

Zakariya
Grade 3, Age 8

Basketball
I see basketball at a basketball court
The ball is hard and bouncy
I am driving a boat
I make a goal
I am sparring with someone
I am playing with my dad
I feel free and happy

Sophia
Grade 3, Age 8

Leaves Falling
I see red roses at the park
I see irises, too
Leaves fall every day

Adrian
Grade 3, Age 8

My Imaginary Pet
If I had an imaginary pet,
then everything won't run out
When I look at him, my eyes sparkle
When I pet him, he gives me rainbows,
and gives my Nintendo switch a computer
When bad kids come, my imaginary pet
powers at attack mode
He can throw turtles out of my Nintendo
switch and fire and ice,
I love everything he gives me.

Eliana
Grade 3, Age 8

The Day Passes By
I see the beautiful sun
The air is in my face
The stars are bright in my face
I see the clouds pass in the sky
I see the afternoon
The sky is pretty
When I sit down on the beach,
the water makes me so happy
I feel brave and happy

Gage
Grade 3, Age 8

My First Things
My first walk
Everybody is excited
My first word
My first sleep
My first school day
My first friend
My first dinner
I remember these first things
I remember being little
I feel emotional

Vincent
Grade 3, Age 8

New York
New York is somewhere
I want to go
I want to see the statue
I want to try the famous pizza
I want to see the cars,
the tall buildings and the places
A lot of people walk in the street
There is so much to see

Kylie
Grade 3, Age 8

I See A Dog
I see dogs from the same height
I dream of having another dog
Run and have fun
When I take a walk, I see two dogs
They are furry
I will be so happy

Soane
Grade 3, Age 8

I Love Fortnite
I see Fortnite
It's a good game
It's a famous game
I see Fortnite at Grandma's, at school
We make friends in Fortnite

Hazel
Grade 3, Age 8

Dream Life
I dream that I'm famous
I see the red carpet
I dream that I have a private jet
I think of buying expensive purses and perfumes
I hear photos clicking
I have a concert
I have a big house and put my perfume on
I feel my sparkle

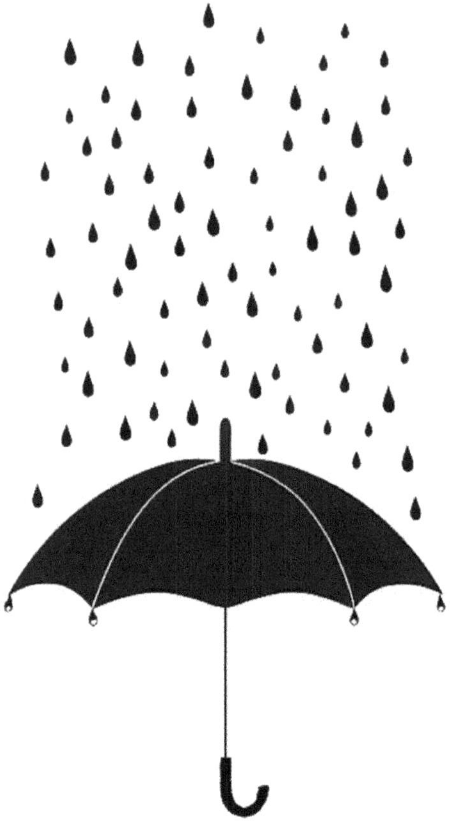

Cata
Grade 3, Age 8

Rain, Rain, Go Away
I can see rain falling from the clouds
I want to play outside
but I don't know why it's raining
My friend wants to play outside
My brother wants to play outside
I am sad
Wait! I think the sun is coming
It is a rainbow
My friend and me
and my brother went outside
I was amazed
There is a rainbow,
perfect and beautiful

Kali
Grade 3, Age 8

A Dog Who Loves Rain
It's raining
A dog loves rain
I love dogs
I see a storm
I see a dog and a cat
Oh, no!

Alma
Age 9, YPL Workshop Student

Rainstorm
Sound of a tornado
Dash of rain, gray clouds
That's a rainstorm

Dayana
Grade 3, Age 8

I See God
I see someone
coming down from the sky
I see God
He says "Hi" to me
I invite him to my house
We drink coffee
He has to leave
and I am sad
He leaves in a ball of light
I go to sleep
It was all a dream

Messiah
Grade 3, Age 8

Space
I see space and its darkness
I smell moon particles
I feel a rocky surface
I see the planets around me
I see the colors of the universe
I see aliens on Uranus
I see a lot of planets
So colorful
I love space

Victoria
Grade 3, Age 8

Art Time!
I like doing art
Water fell into my picture
I could get my mom to help
My mom fixed it
Done with my art
Time to go to sleep
I go to sleep
Tomorrow,
I want to do more art

Leini
Grade 3, Age 8

Fish, Sky
I think about floating fish
but different colors
Fish tails flapping
I see sky so wide
I dream of cotton candy clouds
I feel cotton candy clouds
like a fluffy pillow
I'm laughing and floating in the sky
Saying, "It's so pretty"
Wow!

Alex
Grade 3, Age 8

Soccer
I play soccer
It's the best thing to do
I kick and kick as far as I can
I score goals
When I block a ball,
they scream out my name
We pass the ball, score more goals
I talk to my team, scream to my team,
and win the game

Valeria
Grade 3, Age 8

Beach Sunset
Sunset at the beach
Colors of the sunset
Pink, peach, sometimes blue to the big yellow
People run by the water, brothers and sisters
make sandcastles, boys do flips
Have a picnic with their family
Sun, friends, family, boys and girls
"It's beautiful!" I say

Samantha
Grade 3, Age 8

Me and My Dog
Me and my dog Lily
are playing under the porch
We are playing fetch
She runs to get the ball
Lily brings the ball back
I hear her barking with excitement
We go to the dog park
I love my dog so much
I wish she was better

Leslie
Grade 3, Age 8

Fall Fun
Fall is so fun
Jumping in the leaves,
leaves crunching
I feel really calm when it's fall
I also feel excited when fall starts
There is much to do
Snow angels in the leaves
Dressing in brown and green
I kinda look like leaves
when I wear brown and green

Aileen
Grade 3, Age 8

Float
My dream is to float
I dream of being in the sky
That will make me joyful
I want to sleep in the sky
with clouds so fluffy and soft
I want to touch the clouds
and the star with my hand
That is my dream

Nathalia
Grade 3, Age 8

My Kitty
I love my kitty Minchi
White, black, and gray
"Meow!"
He's so cute and chubby
My parents love him
He's always hungry and sleepy
He loves my bed so much
He loves the pillow the most
He loves to scratch our couch
He's so cute and happy

Kenneth
Grade 3, Age 8

Soccer
I like to play soccer with my friends
on the field
It makes me joyful
I see black-and-white spots
Sometimes we play with an orange ball,
green ball, purple or white ball
I am delighted that I can play with my friends
Sometimes we win and sometimes we lose
but we are always happy

Jayla
Grade 3, Age 8

Birds and Butterflies
I see a blue butterfly on a flower
The wings of the butterfly are soft
I see the bird in the clouds
I hear birds chirping
I walk and see a huge tree and more birds
I keep walking and then I see a lot of butterflies
They are so colorful
I see all the butterflies and birds
It's all beautiful

David
Grade 3, Age 8

Little Brother
I always love to play with my cute little brother
I love to carry my brother
When my brother comes to my room,
I play with him
I love to walk with him
I love when CJ eats with me at breakfast

Anita
Grade 3, Age 8

Me!
It was a good day for Anita...
It was Friday!
She went to school, she went home and finally...
It...was...TIME to go!
A few days with dad and it was time to go back
It was the end of my world!

Juan
Grade 3, Age 8

School Dreams
I watch people come to school
I see people playing together with joy
I feel happy
Maybe I could learn more hard stuff
I try to learn times and reading books
Also, I want to race kids with my new friends
I want to be the fastest kid
And I wish to be a teacher of 12th grade
I am going to feel nervous
Also, I want to play pro soccer
and to be the best player
I feel so scared
And I wish to be on yard duty for lunch
Once I am on yard duty,
I'm going to take good care of kids
I am going to feel kinda happy

Noah
Grade 3, Age 8

My Gaming Dream
When I was 6 years old, I had a dream.
I said, "You know what?"
I had seen many online gaming sites.
They had tons of followers,
so I decided to become one.
I started gaming because my nephew taught me.
On the first day, it wasn't that bad.
I actually liked it.
Now, it's one year playing internet games.
I love it!

When it was two years,
I started my gaming channel.
I didn't make any videos yet because I was lazy.
But think of making one video in October.
I hope one day my work will pay off and
I'll be famous
I will probably donate to charity
or help my family with money.
Because I feel nice.

Julian
Grade 3, Age 8

The Pool
I like being in the pool
with my parents.
Blue water looks like glass.
We play with the sinky rings.
We dive to the bottom to get them.
"I have it!"
I feel happy.

Xavier
Grade 3, Age 8

I am at the water in the waves, wush, wush!
I feel happy when my brothers and my mom go
swimming in the water. I feel relaxed in the water.
I am swimming. Mom says, "we have to go."
I feel sad.

BIOGRAPHIES

Kathleen Herrmann
Vallejo Co-Poet Laureate
(01/01/2024 – 12/31/2024)

Kathleen Herrmann, an educator, holds a Bachelor of Arts with honors in English Literature from the University of California at Berkeley and a Master of Arts in Teaching Leadership from St. Mary's College of California. She is a teaching artist in the Vallejo City Unified School District under VTA (Vallejo Teaching Artists) and is part of the current "Youth Poetry Letters" international project.

Her original work appears in 14 anthologies, including *I Can't Breathe* and *Coming Out Of Isolation* (Kistrech International Poetry Festival, Kenya, 2021, 2022), *Friendship* and *Loss* (Pure Slush, Australia, 2021, 2024), Work & the Anthropocene (Ice Floe Press, Canada, 2022), Poetic Edge Publishers (UK, 2024), B Cubed Press, Moonstone Press, Napa Valley Writers, and Benicia Literary Arts. She has also been published in the *Going The Distance* column in the Benicia Herald. She was awarded Best in Show at the Solano County Fair in 2022 and 2023. She is an occasional guest reader and host on OZCAT radio's Art Beat Poetry Hour.

She has read poetry at Vallejo's Martin Luther King March (sponsored by the NAACP), Black History Month Celebration, Winters LitFest 2, Benicia's Fiestas Primavera, Vallejo's Second Friday Art Walk and Earth Daze Festival, Girls On The Rise: Find Your Place in the Legal Field, sponsored by the Solano Superior Court, Solano Bar Association and Solano Commission for Women and Girls, the Solano County Fair, the Brushstrokes For Earth exhibit,

Vallejo's Mad Hatter July Fourth Waterfront Festival, the Visions of the Wild Festival, and the Mad Hatter Holiday Festival. She co-hosts Tea House Poetry Open Mic with her poetic partner, Jacalyn Eyvonne. Her first poetry book, *Cane In The Sand*, will be released in 2025.

Jacalyn Eyvonne, Vallejo Co-Poet Laureate
(01/01/2024 – 12/31/2024)

Jacalyn's first published poem, "It's Magic," appeared in the Oakland Tribune Newspaper Sports Notebook on November 12, 1991. It was a dedication to Magic Johnson after his HIV announcement. She is the former publisher of *In The Company of Poets Magazine*, with work featured in numerous anthologies, including Hues of Spring Anthology, Hues of Spring Anthology 2, NYRA Publishers, 2024; World Healing World Peace, 2024, Inner Child Press, Holes: An Anthology, JLRB Press, Wheelsong United Kingdom Anthologies 3 and 4, Animal Tales Anthology, Table Rock Poetry Fest, Screaming at America, and Rituals 2024, among several others.

A graduate of the Academy of Art University San Francisco in Motion Picture and Television, she has worked with youth in film under the VTA program.

Activities include YPL Youth Workshops, Poetry Playground, and Youth Poets in the Spotlight. Guest poetry readings and appearances throughout Solano County include the Solano County Supervisor's Juneteenth Flag Raising, Solano County Fair, Mad Hatter Holiday Parade and July 4th Waterfront Festival, Brush Strokes for Earth, Earth Daze Festival, OZCAT Radio, McCune Collection, guest poet at John F. Kennedy Library and Vallejo Naval and Historical Museum's Black History Month, events, including numerous local open mic venues.

She has been featured alongside her poetic partner in the Vallejo Times Herald, Daily Republic, and The Mississippi Link newspaper. Jacalyn Eyvonne's books include *"I Am Not An Inconsequential Word, Poetry and Remnants, The Unyielding Weight of Words, Poems on Reflection, Healing & Love, Venting to Verse - How To Turn Anger Into Poetry,"* and *"Strange Things Happen At Midnight,"* a collection of short weird tales. JacalynEyvonne.com

Vallejo Teaching Artists (VTA)

Vallejo Teaching Artists (VTA) is a local nonprofit organization that provides safe and supportive spaces for the youth of Vallejo to develop and share their artistic craft, express their creative voice confidently, and influence the landscape of social justice.

In partnership with the Vallejo City Unified School District, local teaching artists from VTA offer Vallejo students visual art, dance, music, creative writing, cinematography, graphic design, and theatre lessons; allowing students to experiment with mediums, express their artistic voices, share their work with authentic audiences, and connect to their academic work in a meaningful way.
Funding for this valuable project was provided by Vallejo Teaching Artists and the California Arts Council.
vallejoteachingartists.org; arts.ca.gov

Youth Poetry Letters

www.YouthPoetryLetters.com